ISSUES THAT CONCERN YOU

Foster Care

Other books in the Issues That Concern You series:

ISSUES THAT CONCERN YOU

Foster Care

Jill Hamilton, *Book Editor*

Christine Nasso, *Publisher*
Elizabeth Des Chenes, *Managing Editor*

GREENHAVEN PRESS

An imprint of Thomson Gale, a part of The Thomson Corporation

THOMSON
GALE

Detroit • New York • San Francisco • New Haven, Conn. • Waterville, Maine • London

LIBRARY OF CONGRESS CATALOGING-IN-PUBLICATION DATA

Foster care / Jill Hamilton, book editor.
   p. cm. -- (Issues that concern you)
 Includes bibliographical references and index.
  ISBN-13: 978-0-7377-2711-1 (hardcover)
 1. Foster home care--United States. 2. Foster home care--United States--History.
3. Foster children--Services for--United States. 4. Foster parents--United States. I.
Hamilton, Jill.
 HV881.F644 2007
 362.73'30973--dc22

2007029807

Printed in the United States of America

10 9 8 7 6 5 4 3 2 1

CONTENTS

INTRODUCTION

In the United States, the foster care system has not yet hit upon a perfect solution for dealing with children who, for one reason or another, cannot live with their families. For as long as there have been such children, there have been different ideas of how to care for them, depending on what the popular child-rearing theories of the time are.

The earliest foster care in the United States was little more than an indentured servant program. In the colonies, children without parents were sent to learn a trade. In the 1700s and 1800s, such children were put in publicly run shelters called almshouses. Conditions in such places were poor, and anyone with an interest in a child could take the child with no questions asked. There was no monitoring system in place once the children left the shelter, and the children often became household servants or were abused. The adults were paid by the state to take care of the children and in that sense were the country's earliest foster parents.

In the mid-1800s, two things changed the face of foster care. The first thing was that Charles Loring Brace, a minister and director of the New York Children's Aid Society, devised a program to match homeless children with new homes. The system wasn't perfect—again, many of the children became indentured servants—but it did provide the basis for the modern foster care system. The second big shift was that people started recognizing the importance of using laws and the government to protect children. When a New York City charity worker heard about a particularly scandalous case of foster child abuse, she tried to get the court to intervene. There were no child protection agencies or laws protecting children so she was forced to use the Society for the Prevention of Cruelty to Animals to take her case. Soon afterward, the New York Society for the Prevention of Cruelty to Children was developed. It spurred the formation of other agencies across the nation that were dedicated to keeping children safe.

These foster parents have cared for 100 children over a 25-year span.

By the 1900s, the foster system was improving. Foster agencies worked more closely with foster families. They inspected homes, made follow-up visits, and tried to match children with appropriate families. Children were seen as people who needed to be nurtured and protected rather than just small-sized workers.

By the mid-1970s, the number of children in foster care in the United States was more than one hundred thousand. As the system grew, it suffered growing pains. There were debates over the suitability of gay or single foster parents. People argued over whether it was appropriate to pair children and foster parents of different races. And there was the hard-to-ignore issue that certain children—older ones, those with special needs, and particular minorities—were more likely to languish in the system.

Today the number of children in foster care stands at more than half a million, and our society still has not found the ideal solution for dealing with these children. The system is filled with problems. There are still too many cases of foster child abuse. There are too many children who are hard-to-place due to their special emotional or medical needs. And if such children do get placed, they often don't receive the kind of medical care they need. Foster parents complain of inadequate support systems from foster care agencies and of not receiving adequate financial compensation. Kids can be bumped around from family to family, never getting any sense of stability. The average child in foster care stays three

Some foster parents are willing to take in several children at a time.

years and goes through three home placements. Foster kids are not given enough training to know how to take care of themselves once they "age out" of the system. And once foster children do age out, there is no formal support system for them to rely on.

How should these problems be solved? It depends on whom you ask. Some argue that grandparents are the way to solve the foster care crisis. They point to the large contingent of older Americans who are healthy, willing, and able to parent their children's children. Others argue that removing all barriers to gay people becoming foster parents is key. They note that gay parents could make up for the shortage of available foster parents. Some say that foster care's problems are exaggerated and that the public is simply misinformed about what is really going on in the system. For them, better public education is the key. And recently, the whole idea of a foster care system has been under scrutiny. Adherents to the idea of "family preservation" seek to keep families together whenever possible. They argue that instead of removing children from bad homes, we should work to improve those homes through parent education, agency involvement, and child monitoring.

This anthology contains excerpts from magazine opinion pieces, Web sites, and newspaper articles that cover a variety of viewpoints on how to fix the foster care system. There is also an appendix for the reader who is interested in further exploring the topic of foster care. "What You Should Know About Foster Care" gives readers a quick, itemized look at pertinent facts about foster care. "What You Should Do About Foster Care" offers concrete suggestions for those who would like to take action on the issue. The appendixes also include an extensive bibliography of media sources and a list of organizations to contact. *Issues That Concern You: Foster Care* offers a wide-ranging look at the current issues surrounding the foster care system in America.

ONE

The History of Foster Care in the United States

Ellen Herman

The following selection, taken from The Adoption History Project, details the history of the changes in foster care in the United States. The essay shows that how society has coped with these children is constantly changing, depending on the prevailing wisdom of the times. In 1910, orphanages were the accepted way of dealing with such children, and there were more than one thousand orphanages in the United States. But institutional care started losing favor when people realized that children at orphanages showed a disturbing rate of sickness and death. Many people began to agree with early reformer Henry Dwight Chapin, who said, "A poor home is often better than a good institution." Placing children in homes started gaining favor and, by the 1950s, more children were in homes than in institutions. Over the years, foster care has changed in the face of debates over subsidies, race, hard-to-place children, and problems with children "aging out" of the system.

The Adoption History Project is a Web site created by Ellen Herman, a faculty member of the Department of History at the University of Oregon. Herman calls the project her "effort at public service history."

Ellen Herman, "Fostering and Foster Care," *The Adoption History Project*, online, February 2005. Copyright © 2005 Ellen Herman. Reproduced by permission.

Before 1945, "fostering" referred to numerous arrangements in which children were cared for in homes other than their own. The point of the term was to contrast institutional care with family placements. The case for foster care was articulated by nineteenth-century child-savers, including Charles Loring Brace, publicized by the orphan trains[1], and advanced by states that experimented with placing-out children rather than consigning them to orphanages.

In the early twentieth century, the cause was taken up by reformers like Henry Dwight Chapin, a New York pediatrician and founder of the Speedwell Society whose wife established one of the country's first specialized adoption agencies, the Alice Chapin Nursery, in 1910. Henry Chapin circulated statistics showing that orphanages literally sickened and killed alarming numbers of children. His conviction that "a poor home is often better than a good institution" spread quickly among child welfare and public health professionals, but in 1910, there were well over 1000 orphanages in the United States, and their average size had grown considerably since the late nineteenth century. The campaign to make families the only acceptable places to raise children still had a long way to go.

Early Foster Care

On the front lines of this movement were "foster parents" who took other people's children into their homes temporarily and permanently, informally and formally. Children who earned their keep by working, children whose board was paid by agencies, and children placed in "free homes" were all living in foster families. During the early decades of the twentieth century, legally adopted children were also called foster children. The terms of family care varied enormously. Terminology did not.

Long before "adoption" was commonly used, child-placers appreciated the differences between permanent kinship and

---

[1]Between 1849 and 1929 trains of orphaned children were sent throughout North America. Families interested in the children would come to local train stations to see the orphans.

Excerpt From a 1910s Home Investigation Report Form

THE FAMILY

1. How does it stand as to honesty, morality, and trustworthiness?

2. How does it grade in education?_____ In Intelligence?_____

3. Are they kind hearted and sympathetic?

4. Do they seem generous and liberal in spirit?

5. Does any member of the family use intoxicants?

6. Did you learn of any bad personal faults or habits?

7. Are they frugal and industrious?

8. What is their income?_____ Its source?_____

9. Habits of church going_____ Are they active in church work?_____

10. Did you interview husband?_____ Temperament_____

11. Did you interview wife?_____ Temperament_____

12. Husband's purpose in taking child?

13. Wife's purpose in taking child?

14. Are there children in the Home?_____ How many?_____ Ages?_____

Taken from: Georgia G. Ralph, "Elements of Record Keeping for Child-Helping Organizations"

temporary residence in someone else's home. Most Progressive-era social workers aimed to keep children with their own families, even if they were illegitimate, out of respect for the importance of blood ties. But advocates also knew that some children could not or should not live with their birth parents. For these children, becoming a lifelong member of a new family was desirable. Common sense suggested that emotional security was key to children's health and welfare, and developmental science produced additional evidence for this claim. Research on attachment and loss and studies of maternal deprivation in infancy influenced policies of early placement and ushered in a more pro-adoption climate after 1940.

More Children in Foster Care than in Institutions

By 1950, statistics showed that children in family foster care outnumbered children in institutions for the first time. By 1960, there were more than twice as many in foster care. By the late 1970s, the foster child population exceeded 500,000, roughly where it

Today foster parents are recognized for their commitment to caring for children other than their own, but that hasn't always been the case.

stands today. Foster placements could be numerous and lengthy in practice, but in theory they were temporary because children maintained ties to their birth parents. Between the 1930s and the 1970s, as foster care became more common for more children, adoptions increasingly involved practices like matching [placing children with parents with similar appearance, religious beliefs and intelligence], policies like confidentiality and sealed records, and placements of infants and toddlers rather than older children. Adoption aspired to the wholesale substitution of one family for another. Foster care did not.

Two developments distanced adoption from foster care after the New Deal [1930s] and World War II [1940s]: the growth of public social welfare services and a new consciousness about the plight of African-American, mixed-race, older, native, developmentally delayed, physically disabled, and other hard-to-place children. Anti-poverty programs like Aid to Dependent Children (established by the Social Security Act of 1935 and later renamed Aid to Families With Dependent Children) offered financially struggling parents an alternative to placing their children in institutions or surrendering them forever. When the program expanded in the early 1960s, federal funding for foster care was added. The result was an explosion in out-of-home family placements. During the last half-century, foster care has come to designate this government-funded system. Foster care is now the main form of assistance provided to poor children in the United States who cannot remain in their own homes because of neglect or abuse.

Foster Care and Race

Race as well as class marked the growing gap between foster care and adoption. During the postwar civil rights era, poor children of color, formerly denied many services, comprised more of the foster care caseload. Foster parents were somewhat better off economically than the children in their care, but they too were increasingly drawn from minority racial and ethnic communities. Foster parents were licensed and compensated by the state for the work they did, however meagerly, and had fewer legal protections than adoptive or birth parents. By definition, foster parents were not autonomous. They were expected to provide havens of safety and love for children at risk, but they were also responsible for keeping children in contact with relatives and agency workers. Adopters, on the other hand, were more affluent. They paid for the services they received, overwhelmingly preferred babies and young children whose racial identities matched their own, and were legally entitled to manage their families without supervision after court decrees were issued. Adoption spelled permanence, but the price of that permanence was the social obliteration of natal ties.

Children sometimes moved from foster care to adoption. Because termination of parental rights was a lengthy process, most of these were (and are) special needs adoptions. Foster children were invariably older and had complex loyalties to natal and foster kin. Their histories of separation and trauma were associated with behavioral and health problems. These characteristics made them undesirable to many would-be parents, and that made their adoptions difficult and expensive to arrange. After midcentury, agencies invested scarce time and money recruiting parents for hard-to-place children. By the 1960s, a few turned in frustration to controversial solutions like transracial adoptions.

Foster Care vs. Adoption

Another approach, pioneered by New York state in 1965 and supported by the federal Adoption Assistance and Child Welfare Act of 1980, was to subsidize adoptions. Subsidies exposed the cruelty of market forces by offering economic incentives to adopt children for whom there was little or no demand. They challenged the assumption that permanent kinship required financial independence and acknowledged the high costs of raising children who needed ongoing medical and psychological help. If subsidies began to undercut the differences between foster care and adoption, a 1977 class action suit did just the opposite. In *Smith v. OFFER*, the U.S. Supreme Court decided that foster parents were not entitled to the same constitutional rights as other parents.

Because states licensed, created, and paid them, foster families could not oppose children's removal or expect to remain intact, as birth families could, no matter how long-lasting and deep the ties between foster parents and children.

For the past several decades, the foster care system has confronted substance abuse, AIDS, and other adult epidemics that trickle down to children. Even as more Americans seek healthy infants and toddlers through open adoptions, international adoptions, and new reproductive technologies, foster children drift from one placement to the next, and approximately 20,000 "age out" of the system each year. Their tragic plight has provoked soul-searching about "permanency planning," hearings about barriers to adoption, and legislation, such as the Adoption and Safe Families Act of 1997, that commits new resources to adoption. "Kinship care," which seeks to transform grandmothers, aunts, and other birth relatives into certified foster parents or legal guardians, is one recent response to the failures of foster care. Such policies reflect the enduring rhetoric of family preservation while acknowledging the insurmountable odds against secure belonging for too many American children.

TWO

Public Ignorance Hurts the Foster Care System

Mary Bissell and Rob Geen

In the following selection, Mary Bissell and Rob Geen argue that it isn't the lack of funding that is the problem with foster care, but the public's lack of knowledge about the system. Influenced by lurid and pessimistic media reports, people get a skewed impression of foster care and think the problems are too pervasive to be solved. Bissell and Geen write that the first step to fixing foster care is to educate the public on the truth about foster care. They debunk several prevalent myths about foster care. For instance, well-publicized reports of abuse by foster parents have led to the perception that such abuse is widespread. In fact, of children who experienced abuse or neglect in 2002, 81% were abused by their parents but less than 1% were abused by their foster families. They refute the myth that foster children stay in foster care for a long time. In fact, in 2002, 19% spent less than a month in foster care and 51% spent less than a year.

Bissell is a fellow at the New America Foundation, a public policy group dedicated to promoting new voices and ideas. Geen is the director of the Child Welfare Research Program at the Urban Institute, an economic and social policy research organization.

What prevents the U.S. child welfare system from doing all it can to protect children and support families? Complex social problems? Insufficient funding? Staff turnover? The truth is, the inability to address these barriers is rooted in a much larger problem—a chronic lack of public will. Despite its best efforts, child welfare faces daunting challenges in making policymakers and the public understand and commit to fixing the system.

Child welfare agencies and service providers rarely have the time, expertise, or capital to invest in strategic communications that promote their successes. And media coverage rarely moves beyond crisis-driven headlines to a more meaningful discussion of the programs and policies necessary to stop a crisis before it occurs. The unfortunate result is that the public understands little about foster care—and the information it does have is often based on anecdotes or stereotypes.

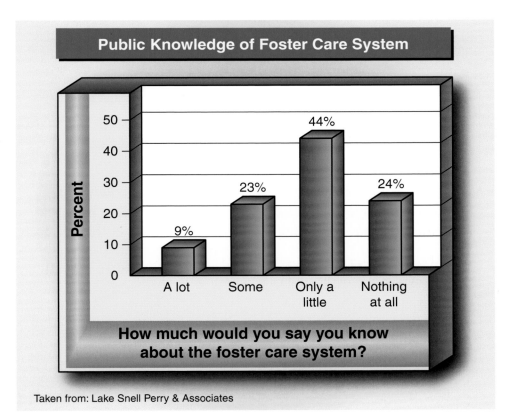

Taken from: Lake Snell Perry & Associates

To build support for child welfare innovations, the public first needs accurate information. The following test is designed to help you educate the opinion leaders in your community to distinguish foster care fact from fiction.

Most abused or neglected children end up in foster care. *FALSE.*

In 2002, more than 3 million children were reported to child welfare agencies for abuse and neglect. About 900,000 of these children were confirmed as victims of abuse and neglect, but only one-fifth were actually placed in foster care, the last resort when they can no longer remain safely with their parents.

In fact, most cases of abuse or neglect aren't serious enough for children to be taken from their families. Instead, child welfare agencies should provide supportive services to stabilize the family. Although child welfare agencies provided these preventive services to more than 1.7 million children in 2002, about 40% of child victims of abuse and neglect received no services at all.

Why Are Kids in Care?

Most children are in foster care because of physical abuse. *FALSE.*

Nearly 58% of children in foster care have been removed from their families for neglect (for example, their parents have left them unsupervised at home or failed to take care of their basic needs). About 19% of all children who are maltreated are physically abused, 10% are sexually abused, and 7% psychologically abused. The remaining 6% of maltreated children experience educational or medical neglect, cases in which a parent fails to ensure that a child goes to school or receives proper medical care.

Foster parents rarely end up adopting the children in their care.
FALSE.

Of the children adopted in 2002, 61% were adopted by their foster parents. Family members adopted another 24%. "Like all parents, foster parents form strong emotional attachments to the children in their care," says Courteney Holden of Voices for Adoption. "Foster parents and children often become forever families by choosing adoption."

There is a national shortage of foster parents. *TRUE*.

With the onset of the crack cocaine epidemic, the number of children in foster care doubled between 1986 and 1996, while the number of available foster care homes declined. "This trend is expected to continue as an increasing number of foster parents adopt children in their care," says Karen Jorgenson of the National Foster Parent Association. "We now need 130,000 more foster homes to meet the demand."

Grandparents and other relatives can't become foster parents.
FALSE.

Increasingly, child welfare agencies are relying on placements with caring relatives for abused and neglected children. Grandparents and other relatives currently provide care for nearly one-third of all children in foster care. "Sometimes, children move through the child welfare system without anyone realizing that the solutions to their care lie right there with the children's families' networks," says CWLA [Child Welfare League of America] President and CEO Shay Bilchik. "Grandparents and other relatives should be the first line of defense."

How Long Are Kids in Foster Care?

Most children stay in foster care or a long time. *FALSE*.

Even a week is an endless amount of time to a child, but most abused and neglected children do not spend their entire childhoods in foster care. Of the children who left foster care in 2002, 19% spent less than a month in foster care, and 51% spent less than a year in care.

Some statistics show that most children who enter foster care don't stay long, but those who do can face challenges moving beyond the system as they become adults with no family support.

Unfortunately, however, more than one-fourth of children in foster care have been there for at least two years, and 17% of children have been in foster care for five years or more. Equally distressing, an estimated 10% of maltreated children who go home to their parents return to foster care within the year.

Most children in foster care move around a lot. *FALSE*.

Although media accounts often focus on the experiences of children with multiple foster care placements, 84% of children who have been in foster care for a year or less have had two or fewer placements (and the first placement often is an emergency shelter). Child welfare agencies have far to go, however, to minimize placement disruptions. "Each additional move after the trauma of children's separation from their families only adds to their sense of loss, confusion, and uncertainty," says consultant Madelyn Freundlich, formerly of Children's Rights Inc.

All children in foster care get federal support. *FALSE*.

A child's eligibility for federal foster care funds is based on whether the child enters care from a low-income family rather than on the child's individual needs. More than 40% of children in foster care are not eligible for federal foster care support. According to Rutledge Hutson of the Children's Defense Fund, "The federal government should have a role in responding to the needs of all children who have been abused or neglected, not just those from very poor families."

Do Siblings Stay Together?

In most cases, siblings in foster care are placed together. *TRUE*.

About 60% of children in foster care are placed together with some or all of their siblings, but it still doesn't happen often enough, according to April Curtis, an Illinois advocate for foster youth. "Agencies also need to do more to help siblings maintain close relationships when they can't be placed together," Curtis notes. "Many states only allow siblings two one-hour visits per month. That adds up to only one day per year."

Foster parents are in it for the money. *FALSE.*

"There's a difference between doing it for the money and needing money to do it," says Margie Chalofsky of Washington, DC's Foster and Adoptive Parent Advocacy Center. "The real question is whether that foster parent is a good parent and the child is well-placed in their home." Foster parents point out that foster care stipends rarely cover even children's basic expenses. Nationally, the average monthly foster care payment for a 9-year-old child is $420. The average middle-class family spends about $780 on a child of the same age, according to the U.S. Department of Agriculture.

Child maltreatment is higher in African American families. *FALSE.*

There is no difference in the incidence of child maltreatment based on race. African American children, however, are significantly overrepresented in foster care, comprising 15% of the U.S. child population, but 41% of the foster care population. "The child welfare system needs to better understand exactly why children of color are disproportionately represented in foster care before we can improve these children's lives," says Ralph Bayard of Casey Family Programs in Seattle.

Abuse by foster parents is rare. *TRUE.*

Whether perpetuated by birthparents, foster parents, or any other adults, child abuse is wrong. Well-publicized tragedies of children abused in foster care, however, often distort public perceptions of the benefits that foster families provide to children who have experienced abuse and neglect before entering foster care. Of children who experienced abuse or neglect in 2002, 81% were abused by their parents, but less than 1% reported abuse by those foster families.

Are Birth Parents Involved?

Foster parents are not permitted to contact a child's birthparents. *FALSE*.

In addition to caring for a child, foster parents can play an important role in helping birthparents enhance their parenting skills and improve their relationships with their children. "Foster parents are often needed as mentors to birthfamilies," explains Chiemi Davis of Casey Family Programs. "More and more frequently, they are becoming key members of a team that can include social workers, relatives, and, of course, the youth."

Child welfare workers earn about the same as public school teachers. *FALSE*.

The average starting salary of a child welfare worker is $22,000, one-third less than the average beginning salary of public school teachers. Given the difficult working conditions and poor compensation, it's no surprise that 22% of child welfare workers leave their jobs every year. The average tenure of a child welfare worker is less than two years.

Child welfare workers have higher caseloads than they should. *TRUE*.

Nationally, average caseloads for child welfare workers are double the accepted standards for good social work practice. In some jurisdictions, caseloads are three to four times the accepted standard.

Most children have bad experiences in foster care. *FALSE*.

"The most negative part of foster care is usually not where you're placed, it's how other people judge you," says Letitia Silva, a senior at the University of Pennsylvania who spent time in foster care. "Too often, people treat children in foster care like they did something wrong."

Although every child's foster care experience is different, it's not always bad. According to the National Survey of Child and Adolescent Well-Being, the first comprehensive study of children in the child welfare system, more than 85% of children in foster care reported they like the people they are living with, feel like part of their foster family, and believe their foster parents care about them.

The U.S. foster care system faces persistent challenges, but real improvements are impossible unless new policies are grounded in a better public understanding of the realities facing child welfare workers, foster families, and children. Until the public can understand the daily challenges of the child welfare system, we will not have policies that allow children and families at risk to reach their full potential.

THREE

Poorly Trained "Helping" Professionals Compound Problems

Richard Delaney

In the following selection, author Richard Delaney, Ph.D., argues that foster care professionals need specialized training to deal with the particular issues of foster care. He cites complaints from foster parents in which helping professionals, not understanding the unusual dynamics of foster families, ended up being ineffectual, or worse, exacerbating problems. In one family, for example, a foster child burned down the town library. Instead of examining the child's history of arson, the counselor focused on the details of the couple's marriage. Delaney offers his suggestions on how foster care professionals should be trained.

Delaney, who holds a doctorate in clinical psychology for Loyola University in Chicago, has been a consultant to foster care parents, caseworkers and childcare agencies for the past twenty-five years.

To work with foster and adoptive parents, helping professionals should have more than one arrow in their quiver. Many professionals believe they can use one approach or generic tools with foster care situations, but that doesn't work. Excellent, truly genuine social workers, counselors, psychiatrists, and other helping professionals often simply do not know much about foster care and special needs adoptions.

Even dedicated, highly skilled professionals may lack familiarity with how to help foster children and families. Unfortunately, these professionals do not fathom the impact a formerly maltreated child may have on the foster family's dynamics. These professionals are unaware of the fact that working with foster children and their families requires special expertise. To our knowledge, there are only two universities in the United States which grant a certificate in foster care specialty to mental health professionals.

Foster Parents Speak Out

Sadly, I receive feedback each year from foster and adoptive parents that they were not only unhelped, but were actually hurt by involvement with helping professionals. No one wants that. Here's what I have been told, "They never listened to my side of the story. The psychologist met with the child alone and swallowed what she said without checking with us."

> *Note: If there are individual psychotherapy sessions with the child, it is important for mental health professionals to confer with foster parents before and after each session to debrief. Without that, treatment may become irrelevant or even harmful. Children are not above presenting their side of the story only, seeking sympathy or projecting blame. Without the corrective input from foster parents, the unsuspecting professional may be led down the primrose path.*

"The counselor told my foster child she didn't have to follow my directions. This counselor never consulted me directly on this. I guess she felt that I was too strict."

> *Note: It is essential for the counselor to shore up the placement, not pull the rug out from beneath it. If the counselor sees the need for change, discussion directly with you, the foster parent, is mandatory.*

Heavy case loads and inadequate training of social workers can make it difficult for foster families to get the assistance and guidance they need.

Blaming the Foster Parents

"We were at first seen as heroes by everyone at the human services department and at the mental health office. But, when we got too exhausted to continue with our child and asked for her to be removed, all of a sudden we were the enemy."

> *Note: It's not uncommon for helping professionals to become exasperated with foster parents who find it necessary to have a child moved for their own safety and well-being. It's tragic when foster parents are blamed for trying, but not succeeding, with a child. I suspect that we lose many foster parents forever when they feel punished for their need to have an overly taxing child removed from their home.*

"The direction that counseling took was mind-boggling. All the questions focused on how our marriage was doing, how we communicated, and how our approaches with the child were all wrong. We felt like we were to blame, though we had done nothing to force the child to burn down the town library. This child had come to our home because he had already burned down his birth family's home and had started playing with fire at his grandmother's house. We wanted someone to help the child get out his anger in words rather than torch our house, but suddenly we were under the microscope."

Note: If helping professionals are unaware of family dynamics in foster care, they may look at any family dysfunction as the cause of the child's problems. For example, if the foster mother looks exasperated or depressed, that's seen as the reason behind the child's problems. If the foster parents disagree on their view of the child, the marital split is seen as the culprit. Helping professionals who are trained specifically would most likely avoid the pitfalls of applying standard family systems theory to the special families created by foster placements.

Keeping the Whole Family Involved

"We never had a clue about what went on behind closed doors. The caseworker never gave us any feedback. The counselor told us the sessions were confidential. Heck, this was a 3-year-old foster child. Confidentiality? We simply wanted some answers and some direction. How should we handle her three-hour long temper tantrums, many of which occurred after therapy sessions or visits by the caseworker. I asked, why all the secrecy?"

Note: Secrecy indeed! We need more honest communication and much greater cooperation between helping professionals and helping parents. Without that—given the level of disturbance among today's foster children—we will inadvertently undermine placement stability and increase placement failures. Our system needs to re-evaluate how confidentiality is employed and misused. To better help their children, foster parents need to be privy to the facts and concerns.

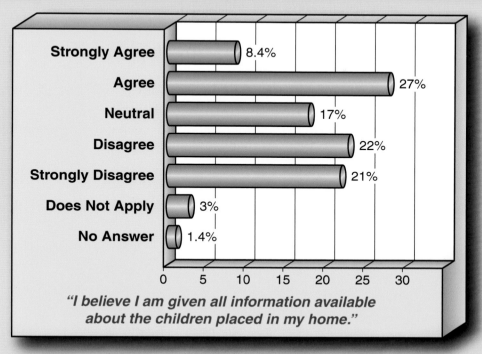

Foster Parent Satisfaction Survey
Professionals Can Help by Providing More Information

Strongly Agree — 8.4%
Agree — 27%
Neutral — 17%
Disagree — 22%
Strongly Disagree — 21%
Does Not Apply — 3%
No Answer — 1.4%

0   5   10   15   20   25   30

"I believe I am given all information available about the children placed in my home."

Taken from: Partnership for Strong Families

Special Training for Foster Care Professionals

If foster parents are to succeed, they deserve specialized, quality mental health services for themselves and their children. For these services to be sound and relevant, the mental health provider needs specific training. Here are some areas of training mental health professionals need:

- Family dynamics in foster care, kinship care and special needs adoptions.
- Special issues related to adolescent mental health in foster care and adoption.
- Helping families raise children who have been drug or alcohol affected before birth.

- Working with families in a team-wise approach rather than emphasizing working with the child in isolation.
- Knowledge of attachment issues—how maltreatment and subsequent foster care drift or multiple placements impairs the child's capacity to attach, trust and relate.
- How to help families design relevant, effective family-based strategies and parenting skills to work with at-risk children.

The chance for successful outcomes for foster and adoptive children will be increased with sound support from helping professionals. These professionals should receive specific training that will ensure the care they offer foster and adoptive families is on target.

FOUR

Homosexuals Should Not Be Foster Parents

J. Richard Pearcey

> J. Richard Pearcey was inspired to write the following selection after seeing a TV show featuring Rosie O'Donnell talking about gay people adopting children and becoming foster parents. Pearcey, a Christian, found the conversation upsetting because he felt O'Donnell was trying to force her beliefs upon others. It is one thing to be gay, he argues, but quite another to insist that the government enact rules that support a "homosexual worldview." Pearcey believes that the normal family structure consists of heterosexual parents and children and that it is cruel to place a child in a situation that differs from the norm.
>
> Pearcey is the editor of Gophers' Den, a blog on the MacLaurin Institute's Web site. The MacLaurin Institute is a Christian study center at the University of Minnesota.

You couldn't ask for a more earnest and sincere advocate of homosexuality and the right of homosexuals to adopt children than talk-show host Rosie O'Donnell. There she was in all her beaming confidence, sitting across from Diane Sawyer for that recent interview on a special two-hour edition of *PrimeTime Thursday*.

The point of it all? *ABCnews.com* put it like this: "Rosie O'Donnell talks about her sexuality with Diane Sawyer—in hopes of shining light on the issues of gay adoption and the plight of 500,000 children in America's foster care system." But for all of O'Donnell's sincerity, it's not all that certain that we should be buying what she's selling.

A few observations.

What Fit Me . . .

The place to start is Rosie's coat, as it were. Rosie used the metaphor of trying on a coat to explain why she is a homosexual. "It took me a while to understand and to figure out all the things that made me me," she said. "Where I was most comfortable, who I was, and how I was going to define my life. What coat fit me. And I found the coat that fit me." So here we have a picture of a very private decision, a very private process, at the end of which O'Donnell says she discovered that a particular coat fit her, and that coat is homosexuality.

But then she jumps from the particular to the universal, and not even Michael Jordan can jump that far. She wants the entire state of Florida to refashion its definition of family so homosexuals can adopt children. She talked about the preparation it takes to become a foster parent—how there is so much to go through to get certified, 30 hours of training, and so on. And she said, "For the state of Florida to tell anyone who's willing, capable and able to do that, that they're unworthy is wrong."

Homosexuals have saturated America with the proposition that homosexuality is a private matter, something people ought to be left alone to decide for themselves. But now suddenly what begins privately and individually for Rosie doesn't stay there, for here she comes telling us that she wants her views to apply to everybody else. It's as if she wants to fit the state of Florida inside her coat, inside the circle of her private struggles and her private definition.

And she's adamant. If the president of the United States says that it's best for children to be adopted into homes where there is a married male and female—well, says O'Donnell, "He's wrong." Not just a little bit wrong, not just a difference in coat size, but "really wrong." And some other people are even worse than "really wrong." They're indulging in "hate-filled" rhetoric. You get the feeling that something more than coat size is at stake here, something more than one person saying she has discovered "how I was going to define my life." . . .

Must Now Fit You . . .

And there is something more, far more. What O'Donnell is advocating is the radical redefinition of America according to the homosexual worldview. Unfair, she might say. "I'm not asking people to accept homosexuality," she said on *PrimeTime Thursday*. "All I'm saying is, don't let these children suffer without a family because of your bias." But clearly this isn't just about preventing children from suffering. For Rosie is asking us to believe that there is no normative family structure. In her interview, she said she has explained to one of her adopted sons that she is the "kind of mommy who wants another mommy." For O'Donnell, "family" can mean lots of mommies or lots of daddies, and she wants the state of Florida to enact this view into policy and have the citizens of Florida abide by her viewpoint and support it with their taxes. To be sure, this is not asking people to become homosexual themselves, but O'Donnell does want them to accept the tenets of the homosexual worldview, and she wants Florida policy to reflect that philosophy. In the world according to Rosie, it's one size fits all, and that size is the size of Rosie's coat.

Bad Fit for Rosie . . .

There's another difficulty we should talk about. It's not just that O'Donnell is trying to enact a homosexual worldview, but also that the "coat" she wants the rest of us to wear is rather ill-fitting—for Rosie herself and for the kids. Rosie does seem ill at ease. For one thing, she described the adoption of one of her children with her "partner" as "when we had a child together." This is a rather curious statement for homosexuals to make; even heterosexuals don't use it when they adopt. Heterosexual procreation is the fundamental norm for human beings, and O'Donnell no doubt feels the pull of her humanity toward the norm. But she must understand that there is no linguistic solution to the fact that homosexuals cannot procreate. She may feel sadness over this, and one can sympathize, but reality doesn't bend to her theory.

Calling something what it isn't doesn't change what it is. We see something similar in the way she refers to her relationship with her "partner." The norm for humanity is that of a male-female relationship in marriage, and Rosie no doubt feels the pull of her humanity toward that kind of relationship too. But by definition she can never enjoy that richness of experience as a homosexual. So again, she resorts to a linguistic device to ease her sense of a lack of fulfillment. She refers to her "partnership" as being one that is "loving," a "life commitment," and so on. But, as in the previous case with her reference to "when we had a child together," the language disguises, instead of describes.

Rosie also uses the word "calling" to describe her mission for homosexual adoption to help the children of Florida. But "calling" in its high and noble connotation speaks of a divine mission from God, and Rosie allows no god but herself to define her identity.

Those who oppose allowing gays to serve as foster parents suggest that children would be at a higher risk for problems in a non-traditional family unit.

Rosie may derive psychological comfort by using such high-flown language to describe what she is doing, but she has given no basis for the belief that God has given her a mandate.

Bad Fit for Kids . . .

If Rosie's language betrays discomfort with her homosexuality, there's also reason to think homosexual adoption is a bad fit for the foster kids of Florida and elsewhere who need to be placed in good homes. Homosexual activists have touted studies purporting to support the notion that kids in homosexual households fare just as well as their heterosexually raised counterparts. But a recent examination of these studies shows that "much of the research fails to meet acceptable standards for psychological research; it is compromised by methodological flaws driven by political agendas instead of an objective search for truth," says researcher Timothy J. Dailey. "Openly lesbian researchers sometimes conduct research with an interest in portraying homosexual parenting in a positive light," Dailey concludes in "Homosexual Parenting: Placing Children at Risk," published by the Family Research Council in Washington, D.C.

The data Dailey has assembled should give pause to people who think homosexual adoption is a viable solution. The indicators of the harmful effects of a homosexual lifestyle are well documented. Dailey examines many studies on homosexual living and finds serious concerns about heightened promiscuity, a significant increase in the risk of incest, the unhealthy aspects of even "monogamous" homosexual relationships, and higher levels of violence, mental-health problems and drug abuse. Such "families" also appear to foster sexual confusion among kids. Dailey notes that a study in *Developmental Psychology* found that "12% of the children of lesbians became active lesbians themselves, a rate which is at least four times the base rate of lesbianism in the adult female population." This suggests that homosexual households could be seen as a recruitment tool for bringing more people in[to] a life of homosexuality—and that they tend to produce that effect whether they intend to or not. (It also, incidentally, challenges the notion that homosexuals are "born that way.")

Homosexuality Puts Kids at Risk

The data are clear: Homosexuality and homosexual households put kids at risk in many ways. The better solution is the one President [George W.] Bush sets forth: Kids need a real mom and a real dad in a real marriage. Sociologist David Popenoe notes the difference that having a mom and a dad makes. "Through their play, as well as in their other child-rearing activities," he writes in *Life Without Father*, "fathers tend to stress competition, challenges, initiative, risk taking and independence. Mothers in their care-taking roles, in contrast, stress emotional security and personal safety." Moreover, "while mothers provide an important flexibility and sympathy in their discipline, fathers provide ultimate predictability and consistency. Both these dimensions are critical," Popenoe concludes, for "efficient, balanced, and humane" child-rearing.

No one is saying heterosexual families are perfect or problem free. And no one is saying that homosexuality, any more than any other sin, is so depraved that its practice excludes one from the human race. That would be false and cruel. But why add to the imperfections of life by placing foster kids in groupings that are fundamentally and structurally flawed? Why deny kids, by law, the fundamental diversity of male and female, of mothers and fathers, they need to grow into healthy individuals and parents themselves? This would be equally cruel.

There is a norm for family, a structure for love. These basics may not fit inside Rosie's coat, but her children need them nevertheless, and no amount of commitment, confidence and skills in parenting can make up for their loss.

FIVE

Foster Kids Have Mixed Feelings About Gay Foster Parents

Represent

There is plenty of debate over whether gay people should be allowed to adopt and to foster children, but rarely are the kids themselves asked what they think about the issue. The editors at *Represent*, a bimonthly magazine written by and for people in foster care, went to Family Support Systems Unlimited in Bronx, New York, to talk about the issue with kids. Six kids in foster care, ranging from age fourteen to nineteen, offered their opinions about gay foster parents. The views ranged from the antigay sentiments expressed by Rashad Matin, sixteen, who thinks that gay people are "automatically going to hell," to the more inclusive Wintai Measho, nineteen, who says, "Why would we kick kids out of a good home just because someone is gay?"

In an editorial meeting at *Represent*, one of our writers in a group home announced, "Everybody knows gay people make the best foster parents. They're the only ones who don't take kids in for the check." Other writers agreed.

So it surprised us to find out that some people feel gay people shouldn't foster or adopt youth. Recently, in Texas, a controversial bill overwhelmingly passed the House to outlaw gay people from becoming foster parents there. Whether the bill becomes a law is still up in the air.

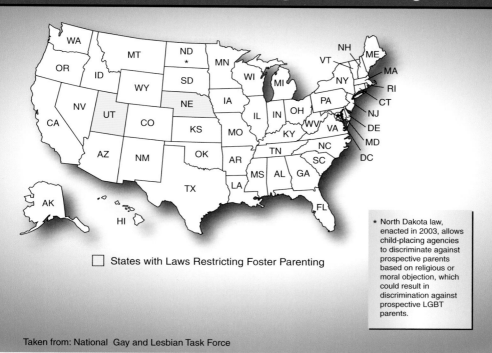

States with Laws Restricting Foster Parenting

★ North Dakota law, enacted in 2003, allows child-placing agencies to discriminate against prospective parents based on religious or moral objection, which could result in discrimination against prospective LGBT parents.

☐ States with Laws Restricting Foster Parenting

Taken from: National Gay and Lesbian Task Force

But other states already have policies or laws to prevent children from living in homes headed by gay people. In Florida, homosexuals can be foster parents, but are prohibited from adopting children. In Nebraska, state policy forbids gays and lesbians from becoming foster parents. In Mississippi, a person who is in a same sex relationship can't adopt—even as a single parent—but a same sex couple can serve as foster parents. Only people who are single or married can become foster parents in Utah: Unmarried couples, straight or gay, cannot foster or adopt.

What Do Kids Think?

Adults make all kinds of laws and policies to keep foster youth away from homosexuals. While there is no evidence or proof that gay people make bad parents, lots of adults feel they are a bad influence on kids. But what do youth in foster care think about having parents who are or might be gay? We went to Family Support Systems Unlimited in the Bronx to find out.

The following teenagers participated in our panel discussion: Earnest Lewis, 14, and his brother Rashad Matin, 16, and Tyrone Nedd, 19, Julio Cirino, 17, Wintai Measho, 19, and Isiah Chase, 16.

Here is what they told us.

Q: Should gays and lesbians be stopped from adopting kids or serving as foster parents?

Julio: No. I think the people who want to stop them are greedy. They must want the checks and the money for themselves. There aren't enough good foster parents now. In a lot of homes the foster parents hit kids, leave 'em in the streets, make 'em eat garbage and lock 'em up instead of letting them go outside. Women who like other women are called lesbians. I think they could even be better foster parents than other women because they wouldn't be bringing all these bad men back home to the house.

Rashad: I just don't like gay people. The Bible is the Bible, and God didn't make two of the same people as a couple. It's important to have exposure to church. If the foster parents are gay, they might not be going to church. (Gay people) are already disobeying the Bible.

It Should Be Up to the Kids

Earnest (grins at Rashad): Is the word (to describe your beliefs) 'homophobia?' The most important thing is to have good foster parents. That's what's most important! A lot of kids are brought up not to like gays, but it should be up to the kids whether they want to live with them or not. If the kids feel living with gay people doesn't hurt them, it shouldn't matter.

Wintai: I'm a youth advocate and I can tell you that before anyone gets approved to be a foster parent they have to be screened. They get fingerprinted and their name is checked against the child abuse registry. Then they have to attend a six-week training. A lot of people get rejected. So if a gay person abused kids or had a criminal record, they would be rejected anyway.

Gay people are the same as regular foster parents, if not better. Why would we kick kids out of a good home just because someone is gay? Or ban anyone from becoming a foster parent for no reason? Besides—what about gay youth? They might feel more comfortable in a gay home because they won't feel judged. Maybe in a gay home they could be themselves.

While society debates allowing gays to serve as foster parents, the children themselves are rarely asked for their opinions.

Tyrone: Maybe (legislators) think that youth wouldn't want gay parents, but it should be up to the youth to decide. I don't think most youth are prejudiced. But to make a law saying they can't be parents—that is prejudice. Texas is a crazy state.

Living with Gay Foster Parents

Q: How would you feel about living in a foster home with parents who are gay or lesbian?

Tyrone: I am afraid of the unknown. But even though I know they're not like me, they're humans just like us. I have to think about it. I've never really known any gay people.

Rashad: It would be like being in jail. If you dropped the soap, you'd have to watch out to see if they'd get at you. I wouldn't care if they were women, but I'd rather have no father than a gay father.

Isiah: It wouldn't matter to me, as long as they don't touch me. I've never known any gay people, but I understand they keep things up. Hygiene is important to me.

Julio: To me the most important thing about any foster parent is whether they can give me respect. Maybe gay people understand this more because they have been disrespected just like kids in foster care. I know this because I hear straight people talk about them behind their backs. They say, "f-ggot" or "he must be gay." Stuff like that.

Earnest: I'd be OK with it, but I don't think I'd be in the house as much. It could be awkward. There are gay kids in my school, but when they talk about hanging out, I don't want to get close to them. On the other hand, I was in one foster home where the lady wouldn't even give me a key and I had to stay outside. I hear a lot about gay people, like they're healthy and clean and like to cook.

Are Gay People Less Likely to Foster for the Money?

Q: Do you agree with our writers who say that gay people might not be as likely to take kids in for the check?

Tyrone: I don't think gay people have more money than other people. Even if they did, that shouldn't matter. Poor people can be good foster parents, too. A placement shouldn't be made based on whether an adult has money, but on whether the child feels comfortable in the home.

Wintai: It's true a lot of (straight) foster parents don't work and are on welfare. I think a lot of gay foster parents and older foster parents aren't as concerned about spending money on their kids. They're more generous. You hear the stories: They'll buy soy milk, Kellogg's cornflakes at $5 a box—anything the kids want!

Rashad: I think they're automatically going to go to hell.

Julio: I think they do have more money, but that's not why they'd be better. If they want to be parents, they can't have their own children. They just want to be parents. That's all they want to do. So they would be taking kids in because they want children.

SIX

Gay Parents Can Solve the Foster Parent Shortage

American Civil Liberties Union of Utah

The American Civil Liberties Union (ACLU) has been a strong advocate of allowing gay people to be parents. The following selection is from the Utah branch of the ACLU. Like many states, Utah faces a shortage of foster parents. Removing barriers to gay foster parents would not only solve that problem, argues the ACLU, but it is also the ethical thing to do. To support their argument, they debunk myths about gay parents. The ACLU contradicts this with a host of studies showing that the sexual orientation of parents has no impact on the sexual orientation of their children. The essay equates gay parents to other groups, such as minorities, older people, and people with disabilities, who in the past faced difficulty adopting or fostering. The ACLU, an organization dedicated to protecting the rights guaranteed in the U.S. Constitution, was founded in 1920 and has more than half a million members.

The last decade [1995–2005] has seen a sharp rise in the number of lesbians and gay men forming their own families through adoption, foster care, artificial insemination and other means. Researchers estimate that the total number of children nationwide living with at least one gay parent ranges from six [million] to fourteen million.

At the same time, the United States generally, and the State of Utah in particular, are facing a critical shortage of adoptive and foster parents. As a result, hundreds of thousands of children in this country, and thousands here in Utah, are without permanent homes. These children languish for months, even years, within state foster care systems that lack qualified foster parents and are frequently riddled with other problems. Here in Utah, the foster care system has done such a poor job of caring for children that it has been under federal court supervision.

Legal and Policy Overview of Lesbian and Gay Parenting

Many states have moved to safeguard the interests of children with gay or lesbian parents. For example, at least twenty-one states have granted second-parent adoptions to lesbian and gay couples, ensuring that their children can enjoy the benefits of having two legal parents, especially if one of the parents dies or becomes incapacitated. [In 2005], the New Hampshire legislature repealed its fifteen-year-old ban on lesbian and gay adoption, after hearing extensive testimony from children's advocates that the policy was misguided.

Recognizing that lesbians and gay men can be good parents, the vast majority of states no longer deny custody or visitation to a person based on sexual orientation. State agencies and courts now apply a "best interest of the child" standard to decide these cases. Under this approach, a person's sexual orientation cannot be the basis for ending or limiting parent-child relationships unless it is demonstrated that it causes harm to a child—a claim that credible social science research simply does not support.

Nonetheless, a few states—relying on myths and stereotypes—have used a parent's sexual orientation to deny custody, adoption, visitation and foster care. Florida remains the only state with a law that expressly bars lesbians and gay men from ever adopting children. The ACLU is challenging that law in a suit filed in May of [2005]. Arkansas, like Utah, passed an administrative policy [in 2004] prohibiting lesbians, gay men, and those who live with them from serving as foster parents. The ACLU is also challenging the Arkansas policy. Thus Utah joins a distinct minority of states that are out of step with national standards and practices in this field, as defined by groups such as the Child Welfare League of America [CWLA].

Research Overview of Lesbian and Gay Parenting

Research to date has reached an unequivocal conclusion about gay parenting: the children of lesbian and gay parents grow up as successfully as the children of heterosexual parents. In fact, not a single study has found the children of lesbian or gay parents to be disadvantaged because of their parents' sexual orientation. Other key findings include:

There is no evidence to suggest that lesbians and gay men are unfit to be parents. Home environments with lesbian and gay parents are as likely to successfully support a child's development as those with heterosexual parents.

Good parenting is not influenced by sexual orientation. Rather, it is influenced most profoundly by a parent's ability to create a loving and nurturing home—an ability that does not depend on whether a parent is gay or straight.

There is no evidence to suggest that the children of lesbian and gay parents are less intelligent, suffer from more problems, are less popular, or have lower self-esteem than children of heterosexual parents.

The children of lesbian and gay parents grow up as happy, healthy and well-adjusted as the children of heterosexual parents.

A Crisis in Adoption and Foster Care

Right now there is a critical shortage of adoptive and foster parents in the United States. As a result, many children have no permanent homes, while others are forced to survive in an endless series

Gay Foster Parents:
A Case Study

Lisa Johnston and her partner Dawn Roginski, both 40, applied to be foster parents to one or more of Missouri's many children in need. Because of their work and volunteer experiences, they were looking forward to giving a home to a child with special needs. When Lisa used to work at a facility for neglected and abused children, she saw lots of children in the foster care system.

"It was so hard seeing these children being bounced around from one placement to another," she said. We have so much love to give to a child, and we decided to try to share some of that love with some of those children who so desperately need it."

So in 2003, when Lisa and Dawn applied for a foster care license, passed a rigorous initial home study, and began attending a training program for prospective foster parents, they thought they should sail through the approval process. Instead, a Department of Social Services (DSS) representative told them that their application for a license was being denied because they are lesbians. Ironically, the couple is far more qualified than most foster care applicants. Lisa works in child development and has a great deal of experience helping abused, neglected, and developmentally challenged children. Dawn is a chaplain at a psychiatric treatment center for children and adolescents with emotional and behavioral disorders, working with children assigned to the center by juvenile courts as well as children who have had difficulty with prior foster care placements. Lisa and Dawn are church leaders and lead a peaceful, home-centered life.

The couple appealed the decision and after losing an administrative appeal, eventually won at the Missouri Circuit Court in April 2006, after a three-year legal battle. The court ruled that there was no basis to deny the license. In response to the court's ruling. DSS agreed to change its policy and now allows lesbians and gay men to apply to foster parent.

Taken from: The American Civil Liberties Union

of substandard foster homes. It is estimated that there are 500,000 children in foster care nationally, and 100,000 need to be adopted. But [in 2004] there were qualified adoptive parents available for only 20,000 of these children. In Utah, notwithstanding efforts to increase the number of placements, the situation has deteriorated, from approximately 3 children for every qualified home in 1995 to more than 4 children for every home in 1998. Many of these children have historically been viewed as "unadoptable" because they are not healthy white infants. Instead, they are often minority children and/or adolescents, many with significant health problems.

There is much evidence documenting the serious damage suffered by children without permanent homes who are placed in substandard foster homes. Children frequently become victims of the "foster care shuffle," in which they are moved from temporary home to temporary home. A child stuck in permanent foster care can live in 20 or more homes by the time she reaches 18. It is not surprising, therefore, that long-term foster care is associated with increased emotional problems, delinquency, substance abuse and academic problems.

In order to reach out and find more and better parents for children without homes, adoption and foster care policies have become increasingly inclusive over the past two decades. While adoption and foster care were once viewed as services offered to infertile, middle-class, largely white couples seeking healthy same-race infants, these policies have modernized. In the past two decades, child welfare agencies have changed their policies to make adoption and foster care possible for a much broader range of adults, including minority families, older individuals, families who already have children, single parents (male and female), individuals with physical disabilities, and families across a broad economic range. These changes have often been controversial at the outset. According to the CWLA, "at one time or another, the inclusion of each of these groups has caused controversy. Many well-intended individuals vigorously opposed including each new group as potential adopters and voiced concern that standards were being lowered in a way that could forever damage the field of adoption."

As a result of the increased inclusiveness of modern adoption and foster care policies, however, thousands of children now have homes with qualified parents.

Myths vs. Facts

Myth:
The only acceptable home for a child is one with a mother and father who are married to each other.

Fact:
Children without homes do not have the option of choosing between a married mother and father or some other type of parent(s). These children have neither a mother nor a father, married or unmarried. There simply are not enough married mothers and fathers who are interested in adoption and foster care. [In 2004] only 20,000 of the 100,000 foster children in need of adoption were adopted, including children adopted by single people as well as married couples. Our adoption and foster care policies must deal with reality, or these children will never have stable and loving homes.

Myth:
Children need a mother and a father to have proper male and female role models.

Fact:
Children without homes have neither a mother nor a father as role models. And children get their role models from many places besides their parents. These include grandparents, aunts and uncles, teachers, friends, and neighbors. In a case-by-case evaluation, trained professionals can ensure that the child to be adopted or placed in foster care is moving into an environment with adequate role models of all types.

Myth:
Gays and lesbians don't have stable relationships and don't know how to be good parents.

Fact:

Like other adults in this country, the majority of lesbians and gay men are in stable committed relationships. Of course some of these relationships have problems, as do some heterosexual relationships. The adoption and foster care screening process is very rigorous, including extensive home visits and interviews of prospective parents. It is designed to screen out those individuals who are not qualified to adopt or be foster parents, for whatever reason. All of the evidence shows that lesbians and gay men can and do make good parents. The American Psychological Association, in a recent report reviewing the research, observed that "not a single study has found children of gay or lesbian parents to be disadvantaged in any significant respect relative to children of heterosexual parents," and concluded that "home environments provided by gay and lesbian parents are as likely as those provided by heterosexual parents to support and enable children's psychosocial growth." That is why the Child Welfare League of America, the nation's oldest children's advocacy organization, and the North American Council on Adoptable Children say that gays and lesbians seeking to adopt should be evaluated just like other adoptive applicants.

Do Gay Parents Make Kids Gay?

Myth:

Children raised by gay or lesbian parents are more likely to grow up gay themselves.

Fact:

All of the available evidence demonstrates that the sexual orientation of parents has no impact on the sexual orientation of their children and that children of lesbian and gay parents are no more likely than any other child to grow up to be gay. There is some evidence that children of gays and lesbians are more tolerant of diversity, but this is certainly not a disadvantage. Of course, some children of lesbians and gay men will grow up to be gay, as will

Some people feel that allowing gays to serve as foster parents is good for all. The couple get to be parents and the children find a home where they are wanted.

some children of heterosexual parents. These children will have the added advantage of being raised by parents who are supportive and accepting in a world that can sometimes be hostile.

Myth:
Children who are raised by lesbian or gay parents will be subjected to harassment and will be rejected by their peers.

Fact:
Children make fun of other children for all kinds of reasons: for being too short or too tall, for being too thin or too fat, for being of a different race or religion or speaking a different language. Children show remarkable resiliency, especially if they are provided with a stable and loving home environment. Children in foster care can face tremendous abuse from their peers for being parentless. These children often internalize that abuse, and often feel unwanted. Unfortunately, they do not have the emotional support of a loving permanent family to help them through these difficult times.

Gay People Not More Likely to Molest

Myth:
Lesbians and gay men are more likely to molest children.

Fact:
There is no connection between homosexuality and pedophilia. All of the legitimate scientific evidence shows that. Sexual orientation, whether heterosexual or homosexual, is an adult sexual attraction to others. Pedophilia, on the other hand, is an adult sexual attraction to children. Ninety percent of child abuse is committed by heterosexual men. In one study of 269 cases of child sexual abuse, only two offenders were gay or lesbian. Of the cases studied involving molestation of a boy by a man, 74% of the men were or had been in a heterosexual relationship with the boy's mother or another female relative. The study concluded that "a child's risk of being molested by his or her relative's heterosexual partner is over 100 times greater than by someone who might be identifiable as being homosexual, lesbian, or bisexual."

Myth:
Children raised by lesbians and gay men will be brought up in an "immoral" environment.

Fact:
There are all kinds of disagreements in this country about what is moral and what is immoral. Some people may think raising children without religion is immoral, yet atheists are allowed to adopt and be foster parents. Some people think drinking and gambling are immoral, but these things don't disqualify someone from being evaluated as an adoptive or foster parent. If we eliminated all of the people who could possibly be considered "immoral," we would have almost no parents left to adopt and provide foster care. That can't be the right solution. What we can probably all agree on is that it is immoral to leave children without homes when there are qualified parents waiting to raise them. And that is what many gays and lesbians can do.

SEVEN

Foster Kids Need an Alumni Group

Bill Stanton

In the following selection, writer Bill Stanton, a former foster child, challenges fellow foster care graduates to join him in forming a foster care alumni group. He relates his own shame and secrecy about his foster care background and subsequent reluctance to "come out" as a foster kid. He argues that successful adults who came from the foster system should make themselves known to their communities, thus giving foster kids positive role models. This would help balance the negative coverage that media often gives to unsuccessful foster care graduates. Stanton is the director of the Dependent Children's Service Division of the Arizona Supreme Court.

It seems like we can't pick up the paper or turn on the television these days without reading or hearing about a child who has been abused or neglected by their parents. These stories range from a child welfare agency losing a child in the system to children being kept in cages.

Do people ever think about what happens to these children? Where will that child be five years, 10 years, 20 years from now?

Surprisingly, I find that most people really don't give this a whole lot of thought. Abuse of children by their parents is not something that we want to believe happens every second in

America, especially at Christmas time. We are shocked when it is reported, but most often we want to forget about it and move on with our lives.

Today, there are more than 12 million adults in America who "graduated" from the foster care system. We hardly hear about these individuals. Some children leave foster care with many troubles and end up homeless for a time, in mental-health hospitals or in prison. But many former foster children move on in life, become successful and have families.

So why don't we hear about the successes? Is it because those foster children, now adults, were programmed not to talk about their experiences in foster care?

Past Stigma

Go back in time to the 1950s, '60s or '70s, and think about how families were structured. What happened in the family was supposed to stay in the family. When things got so bad that a child was removed from the home, it was a thing of shame. It was a stigma.

A Grim Future for Foster Care "Graduates"

- Fewer than 10% of foster youth enroll in college.

- Unemployment rates for emancipated youth are estimated at 50%.

- Nearly a third of foster children will become homeless at some time within the first year after they leave the system at age 18.

- About one fourth of these youth will be incarcerated within the first two years after they leave the system.

- Approximately one third of foster children will be on public assistance shortly after aging out of the system.

Taken from: Children's Law Center of Los Angeles

Connections with other adults who were foster children may provide beneficial support networks to those who transition from the system into adulthood without families to assist them.

As a child, you certainly didn't want to tell anyone you were a foster child. I can recall this firsthand. Growing up in foster care in the 1960s and '70s, I didn't dare tell anyone I was a foster child. If anyone found out, I was ostracized. Parents wouldn't allow their children to play with me because I was "the foster kid."

Teachers often reacted in one of two ways. They would either immediately label me as the "bad" kid, or they would pity me or not challenge me. Either way, I was an outsider.

I can recall vividly a girlfriend's parent telling me that "her daughter was not allowed to date a foster kid."

So it is no wonder that you don't hear about foster children who have grown up, have families and are successful. Even as adults, many of us don't want to talk about it.

This is a travesty. We—who have been there, done that—can offer so much to the children who are now in foster care.

Still a Stigma Today

Today's foster children are often still labeled, and most don't dare let people know they are a foster child. In addition, just like 30 or 40 years ago, no matter how bad the abuse may have been, most foster children hold on to the hope that someday they can go home, that someday their parents will get better.

[In 2003] at the age of 43, I received a call that my biological mom passed away. My first emotion was not grief. My first thought was, "Wow, I guess I really am never going home," and because of this, my first emotion was sadness.

Here I am, an adult with a family, somewhat successful—and somewhere deep inside I never let go of that hope. Foster children today hold onto that same hope.

Think about the benefit foster children could have if we "alumni" of foster care stepped forward and spent a little time with abused and neglected children. Think of the impact we could have if we were the people they look up to because we lived through what they are living through.

Maybe it is time to stop thinking of ourselves as "former foster kids" but rather as "foster alumni." We really have so much to offer and should take pride in what we survived. We need to give this generation of foster children the hope that so many of us didn't have.

Reaching Out to Youth

There are so many organizations that are looking for volunteers to reach out to foster children. Organizations such as In My Shoes, Inc., (www.inmyshoesinc.org) the Foster Care Review Board (supreme.state.az.us/fcrb/), and Court Appointed Special Advocate (supreme.state.az.us/casa) programs were developed to make the lives of foster children better.

Through our experience as foster care alumni, we have paved a path to success. Now, let's guide the next generation of foster youth down that path so that they can set the example for future generations.

So, next time you hear the question: What happens to foster children when they grow up?, stand tall, speak out and let people know that some of the leaders in our community are foster care alumni.

EIGHT

Grandparents Can Cure Foster Care Problems

Gerard Wallace

"The nation's foster care system is unquestionably broken," Pew Commission chairman Bill Frenzel has said. The solution to foster care problems is obvious, suggests Gerard Wallace. He argues that instead of spending more money to fix a sys- tem that doesn't work, we should turn to the vast and largely untapped resource of grandparents. There are 77 million grandparents in America, and they are living longer, more vital lives. "This national resource is made up of mature, stable and unselfish people," Wallace writes. "They parent again, not for money, but for love." The problem, he argues, is that the child welfare system and laws don't yet provide grandparents with the support that they need. He recom- mends programs that help local grandparents and give them the proper support and legal protection they would need to become primary caregivers. Wallace is the director of the Grandparent Caregiver Law Center at the City University of New York's Brookdale Center on Aging.

More than \$7 billion is spent each year to rescue children from abuse and neglect, but the effort is a failure. The federal government's audits, and now the report of the Pew Commission on Children in Foster Care, all document that children are losing. As Pew Commission Chairman Bill Frenzel stated, "The nation's foster care system is unquestionably broken." The report recommends fixing the "system." But, despite repeated efforts over several decades, no remedy has worked. Why will any work now? Perhaps it's time to stop trying.

The nation already has another child welfare system— one that works. The broken official "system," if it can be called that, has tens of thousands of bureaucrats, volumes of statutes, squadrons of lawyers and the "unseen" partnership of the nation's courts. The other system has no bureaucracy, hardly any statutes and only a handful of attorneys, and it is often at odds with the courts. The broken system cares for 500,000 children, the other for almost 5 million. One ruins children, the other saves them. The system that works is, simply, America's grandparents.

According to the 2000 Census, more than 2.5 million grandparents are solely responsible for their grandchildren. Many more are willing to care for their grandchildren. This national resource is made up of mature, stable and unselfish people. They parent again, not for money but for love.

Grandparents Living Longer

For the first time in history, parents are not the only generation capable of caring for the next. Social and medical advances over the past 100 years have added almost 30 years to our lives. We are now living with vitality and good health into our eighties. Thirty years means that America's 77 million grandparents can become the backbone of a successful child welfare system.

Full use of the nation's grandparents is the only cure for the sickness of foster care. Many of the half-million children left in foster care could live with their grandparents, but so far laws and policies do not put time and money into finding grandparents and enabling them to be caregivers.

The reason is simple: Grandparents are the new kids on the block. Traditionally only parents and the state were entitled to care for children. While parents have numerous legal protections, for more than 100 years case law has given grandparents only a

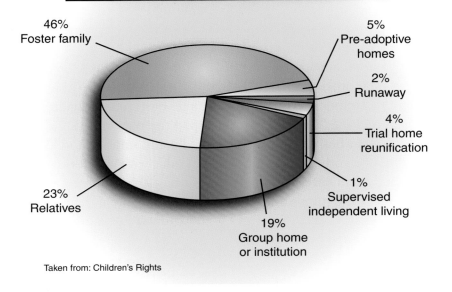

Placement Settings of Children in Foster Care

46% Foster family

5% Pre-adoptive homes

2% Runaway

4% Trial home reunification

1% Supervised independent living

19% Group home or institution

23% Relatives

Taken from: Children's Rights

moral right regarding family matters. Given the current epidemic of child abuse and neglect, what was unassailable a century ago cannot be sustained today. Aside from parents, the state alone has the power to protect children. But, as the Pew Commission report notes, state protection just isn't working.

Grandparents are not in conflict with parents or the state. On the contrary, they are natural allies. As one grandparent said, "When parents can't parent, grandparents can." Indeed, the June 2000 Report to Congress on Kinship Foster Care emphatically declares that kin should be the primary resource for children who cannot remain with their parents.

Incredibly, however, judges have rejected the principle that grandparents are the natural substitute guardians for children. The child welfare system and its ally, the court system, refuse to acknowledge what common sense and our traditions affirm. The results of their entrenchment are tragic. When children are removed from parental homes, they can wind up in the care of strangers.

Improved medical and health conditions are allowing people to live longer which means that grandparents may be able to step in and raise their grandchildren rather than placing them in foster care.

A Need for Pro-Grandparent Laws

Instead of fixing the foster care system, we should make laws that enable grandparents to become caregivers. Arguments that there is no legal foundation for grandparent caregiver rights are in error. In *Moore v. City of East Cleveland* and in *Troxel v. Granville*, the Supreme Court has acknowledged that grandparents have constitutional protections similar to those of parents.

Lawmakers must change direction. Sen. Hillary Rodham Clinton (D-N.Y.) is introducing a bill that would provide federal funding for programs that support these caregivers. New Jersey's Kinship Navigator program offers information and referral, child care, financial assistance, and guardianship subsidies. New York's Grandparent Caregivers' Rights Act gives grandparents a chance to keep their grandchildren and mandates that the "system" inform all grandparents when children are placed in state care. These efforts and others must replace the existing "system."

As the slogan of the National Committee of Grandparents for Children's Rights Declares, "Children from broken homes should not have to lead broken lives." Unfortunately, they'll continue to lead broken lives if we just keep on trying to fix the broken child welfare "system."

NINE

Foster Care Funding Needs Changes

The Economist

The following essay argues that foster care problems in the United States are largely caused by the way that federal funds are allocated. There is not enough money devoted to child services and the little money that is allocated is not used effectively. Many child care issues are pushed into family court, an expensive and time-consuming way to solve problems. The author argues that federal funding is structured to prevent states from providing better care, since they are not allowed flexibility in how they will spend federal funds. The author argues that states should decide how they will spend the money. Flexibility would allow the states to work on keeping children with their families instead of herding them into the foster system. A range of services, including those that could offer help to families while they are still intact, could help reduce the amount of children entering foster care in the first place. The following essay appeared in the *Economist*, a British periodical focusing on business and world affairs.

The budget bill passed [in 2005] by the House of Representatives includes around $50 billion in spending cuts, many of them aimed at federal programmes for the poor. This includes trims of around $5 billion in child support, $600m [million] for children in foster care and around $700m in food stamps. A similar bill from the Senate contains $34 billion of cuts with far fewer swipes at social-welfare programmes, but both bills include between $60 billion and $70 billion in tax cuts that disproportionately favour the rich. Child advocates are enraged. As states consider reforming their child-welfare systems, big cuts in social services are not helpful.

Tales of missing, starved, abused and even murdered children in adopted homes and foster shelters are alarmingly common. Some escape the attention of over-burdened social workers; others are shuttled from one foster-care placement to another for years on end. [In 2005], a Pew Commission on Children in Foster Care concluded that, because of the way federal funding works,

Talking with former foster children may help identify areas where the foster care system should be changed.

children were plucked from their families too soon and left to fester in the system for too long. And although judges play a critical role in moving children to safety, family courts are among the most under-funded in the system, with few incentives to attract top lawyers and judges and little collaboration between the courts and child-welfare agencies. Dependency lawyers tend to be overworked and underpaid, with predictably bad results for the children they represent.

More than 500,000 children are in foster care in America, most of them black or Latino. They remain in the system for an average of three years. These children, typically placed in the state's care after suffering abuse and neglect at home, often endure a demoralising parade of indifferent caseworkers, lawyers, judges, teachers and foster parents, who offer little real support in their quest for a stable home. For those who cannot return to their birth parents, the situation is grim: in 2003, 119,000 children in America were waiting to be adopted, 67% of whom had been in foster care for more than two years, according to the Department of Health and Human Services (HHS).

When such children "age out", or turn 18, as 18,000–20,000 do every year, they are suddenly cut off from all special services such as housing and counselling. Studies show that they disproportionately drop out of college, become homeless and unemployed, turn to drugs and alcohol and spend time in jail.

State Are Not Meeting Basic Standards

The federal government pays around half America's $22 billion child-welfare bill, according to the Urban Institute; the rest comes from state and local governments. But states have not been held accountable for how they spend this money. In an extensive three-year audit of state child-welfare systems, the HHS found that not a single state was in compliance with federal safety standards. When it came to the seven federal standards used to assess children's programmes, some of which are almost embarrassingly basic (eg, "Children are first and foremost protected from abuse and neglect" and "Children receive adequate services to meet their physical and mental health needs"), 16 states did not meet any of them, and no state met more than two. The federal agency is now running a second round of audits, to assess whether states are now complying with their own improvement plans.

"We are spending a great deal of money to damage children," says Marcia Robinson Lowry, director of Children's Rights, an advocacy group. There are no real consequences for states when they fail to meet federal targets, she argues, so class-action lawsuits are the only recourse. Children's Rights has represented foster children in 13 court cases in the past decade. Most of these have ended in a court-ordered settlement that sets the group as a watch-dog over a state's mismanaged and overburdened social-services department.

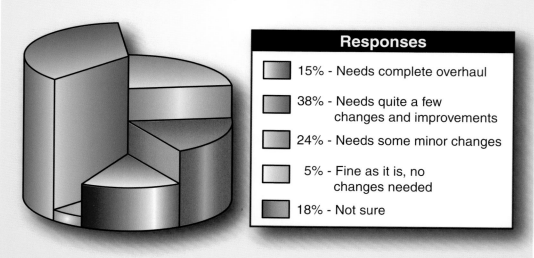

Should the Foster Care System be Changed?

Based on your knowledge of the foster care system, would you say that this system needs a complete overhaul, needs quite a few changes and improvements, needs only some minor changes, or is fine as it is and needs no changes?

Responses

- 15% - Needs complete overhaul
- 38% - Needs quite a few changes and improvements
- 24% - Needs some minor changes
- 5% - Fine as it is, no changes needed
- 18% - Not sure

Taken from: Pew Commission on Children in Foster Care

Better Ways to Spend the Money

But using the courts to solve America's child-welfare problems is expensive and inefficient. The best answer, many think, is for states to spend money on keeping families together, by investing in services such as child care and counselling, rather than putting children in care. This would require allowing states to use federal funding in different ways. Most federal dollars now begin flowing to states only when children are removed from their families, giving states a perverse incentive to keep children in foster care, explains Carol Emig, the director of the Pew Commission. Instead, the commission suggests that states need a little more federal money to cover all children, not just poor ones, and the flexibility to create a range of services that might keep children from entering care or help them leave care safely.

Such a change carries quite a price-tag: $5 billion over ten years. But advocates say it will bring long-term savings by producing better educated, less delinquent children and more united families. If states safely reduce their foster-care rolls, they can then reinvest dollars earmarked for foster care in other child-welfare services. Meanwhile, federal reviews will hold states to their programme promises. President George Bush has proposed, alternatively, that states should convert their foster-care entitlement programmes into block grants. That would give flexibility at first, but, over time, it would amount to a cut in funds.

States and cities can already apply for waivers from federal funding restraints; some 20 states have waivers now. Advocates of flexible funding point to Illinois, a waiver recipient, where the foster-care population has been cut in half and adoptions have more than doubled since 1997. And in late October officials in New York City announced that the number of children in foster care has dropped to around 18,000, half of what it was [in 2000]. Once home to one of the worst foster-care systems in the country, the city now works to keep families intact and help them look after their children rather than taking the youngsters away. As a result, "the spigot coming into the system has been narrowed", explains David Tobis, director of the Child Welfare Fund, a local organisation. The money saved from federal entitlements—an estimated $27m in the fiscal year that began in July [2006]—will be put back into preventive services.

October also saw Arnold Schwarzenegger, California's governor, sign into law a number of bills to help the state's foster children—more than 80,000 of them. Most of the new laws will help teenagers when they turn 18, by making sure they stay in college and have somewhere to live.

Amid all the horror stories, it can be easy to lose sight of the people who make foster care work. After describing the madness of waiting all day at court to represent a client, only to receive five minutes of a distracted judge's time, one social worker goes on to describe some of the good foster parents she has met. Her voice grows tender when she describes one couple who have taken in a young, physically disabled child. "You tend to hear about the system's flaws," she explains. "But there are also so many other amazing things."

TEN

Family Preservation Is Safer than Foster Care

National Coalition for Child Protection Reform

In the following viewpoint, an issue paper released by the National Coalition for Child Protection Reform, the authors argue that keeping a child in a troubled home is safer than removing the child. Foster care is unsafe, they argue, offering various case studies as proof. A better way to help a child, they maintain, is to set up intensive family preservation programs. Such programs focus on working with the family over a long period of time and providing education on topics like parenting skills, child behavior, family interactions and safety. They point to the family preservation systems in Alabama and Pennsylvania as models of successful programs.

The National Coalition for Child Protection Reform was formed by professionals in the child welfare system who want to reform policies on child abuse, foster care, and family preservation.

At the heart of the criticism of family preservation is one overriding assumption: If you remove a child from the home, the child will be safe. If you leave a child at home the child is at risk. In fact, there is risk in either direction, but intensive family preservation programs have a better record of safety than foster care.

National Coalition for Child Protection Reform, "Foster Care Vs. Family Preservation: The Track Record on Safety," August 20, 2005. Reproduced by permission.

To understand why, one must first understand one fundamental fact about foster care: It's not safe. Here's how we know:

National data on child abuse fatalities show that a child is nearly twice as likely to die of abuse in foster care as in the general population.

A study of reported abuse in Baltimore, found the rate of "substantiated" cases of sexual abuse in foster care more than four times higher than the rate in the general population. Using the same methodology, an Indiana study found three times more physical abuse and twice the rate of sexual abuse in foster homes than in the general population. *In group homes there was more than ten times the rate of physical abuse and more than 28 times the rate of sexual abuse as in the general population,* in part because so many children in the homes abused each other.

Abuse in Foster Homes

Those studies deal only with reported maltreatment. The actual amount of abuse in foster care is likely to be far higher, since agencies have a special incentive not to investigate such reports, since they are, in effect, investigating themselves.

- In a study of investigations of alleged abuse in New Jersey foster homes, the researchers found a lack of "anything approaching reasonable professional judgment" and concluded that "no assurances can be given" that *any* New Jersey foster child is safe.
- A lawyer who represents children in Broward County, Florida, says in a sworn affidavit that over a period of just 18 months he was made personally aware of 50 instances of child-on-child sexual abuse involving more than 100 Broward County foster children. The official number during this same period: Seven—because until what the lawyer called "an epidemic of child-on-child sexual abuse" was exposed, the child abuse hotline didn't accept reports of such abuse.
- Another Baltimore study, this one examining case records, found abuse in 28% of the foster homes studied—more than one in four.

- A study of cases in Fulton and DeKalb Counties in Georgia found that among children whose case goal was adoption, 34% had experienced abuse, neglect, or other harmful conditions. For those children who had recently entered the system, 15% had experienced abuse, neglect or other harmful conditions in just one year.
- A study of foster children in Oregon and Washington State found that nearly one third reported being abused by a foster parent or another adult in a foster home.

Even the Best Foster Programs Not Immune

- Even what is said to be a model foster care program, where caseloads are kept low and workers and foster parents get special training, is not immune. *When alumni of the Casey Family Program were interviewed, 24% of the girls said they were victims of*

What Are the Case Goals of Children in Foster Care?

Goal	Percent
Reunify with Parent(s) or Principal Caretaker(s)	48%
Live with Other Relative(s)	5%
Adoption	20%
Long Term Foster Care	8%
Emancipation	6%
Guardianship	3%
Case Plan Goal Not Yet Established	10%

Taken from: U.S. Department of Health and Human Services

Some who support foster care reform believe that it is more cost effective and better for the children if support is provided to help families learn how to address problems without removing children from the home.

actual or attempted sexual abuse in their foster homes. Furthermore, this study asked only about abuse in the one foster home the children had been in the longest. A child who had been moved from a foster home precisely because she had been abused there after only a short stay would not even be counted. Officials at the program say they have since lowered the rate of all forms of abuse to "only" 12%, but this is based on an in-house survey of the program's own caseworkers, not outside interviews with the children themselves.

This does not mean that all, or even many, foster parents are abusive. The overwhelming majority do the best they can for the children in their care—like the overwhelming majority of parents, period. But the abusive minority is large enough to cause serious concern. And abuse in foster care does not always mean abuse by foster parents. As happened so often during the Illinois Foster Care Panic for example and as the Indiana study shows, it can be caused by foster children abusing each other.

Compare the record of foster care to the record of family preservation.

The original Homebuilders program [a program designed to help families learn to solve their problems] *has served 12,000 families since 1982. No child has ever died during a Homebuilders intervention, and only one child has ever died afterwards, more than a decade ago.*

Michigan has the nation's largest family preservation program. The program rigorously follows the Homebuilders model

Since 1988, the Michigan family preservation program has served 90,000 children. During the first two years, two children died during the intervention. In the decade since, there has not been a single fatality. In contrast, when Illinois effectively abandoned family preservation, there were five child abuse deaths in foster care in just one year. That's one reason the state subsequently reversed course.

Several states and localities that have bucked the national trend and embraced safe, proven programs to keep families together also have improved child safety.

A Surprising Success: Alabama

One state that is leading the nation in reforming child welfare is the last state many people might expect: Alabama.

But Alabama is implementing a consent decree (*R.C. v. Hornsby*) resulting from a federal lawsuit requiring it to reframe its whole approach to child welfare by following family preservation principles.

Even with an increase in removals in recent years due to methamphetamine, Alabama still removes children at one of the lowest rates in the nation. But re-abuse of children left in their own homes has been cut by 60%—to less than half the national average.

An independent, court-appointed monitor concluded that children in Alabama are safer now than before the system switched to a family preservation model. The monitor wrote that "the data strongly support the conclusion that children and families are safer in counties that have implemented the R.C. reforms."

How Pittsburgh Improved

Another leader is the county-run system in Pittsburgh and surrounding Allegheny County, Pa.

In the mid-1990s, the child welfare system in Pittsburgh was typically mediocre, or worse. Foster care placements were soaring and those in charge insisted every one of those placements was necessary.

New leadership changed all that. Since 1997, the foster care population has been cut by 30%. When children must be placed, more than half of children placed in foster homes stay with relatives, and siblings are kept together 80% of the time.

They've done it by tripling the budget for primary prevention, doubling the budget for family preservation, embracing innovations like the Annie E. Casey Foundation's Family to Family program, and adding elements of their own, such as housing counselors in every child welfare office, so families aren't destroyed because of housing problems.

And, as in Alabama, children are safer. As the foster care population has fallen, re-abuse of children left in their own homes also has declined and there has been a dramatic, sustained drop in child abuse fatalities.

Illinois also has improved child safety, even as it dramatically reduced its foster care population.

Why It Works

There are three primary reasons for the better safety record of communities that embrace safe, proven programs to keep families together:

- Most of the parents caught in the net of child protective services are not who most people think they are.

- When child welfare systems take family preservation seriously, foster care populations stabilize or decline. Workers have more time to find the children who really do need to be placed in foster care.

- Family preservation workers see families in many different settings for many hours at a time. Because of that, and because they are usually better trained than child protective workers they are far more likely than conventional child protective workers to know when a family can't be preserved—and contrary to stereotype, they do place child safety first.

ELEVEN

Group Homes Do Not Teach Kids How to Live on Their Own

Kareem Banks

Kareem Banks went into a group home at age ten and stayed there for seven years. "Living in a group home was like living in a scared straight program," he writes, referring to the fear-tactics-based program used to keep youth from crime and prison. But the bullies and the thieves at the home were not a surprise to Banks, who had heard stories about group homes. What was shocking to him was the lack of life skills the home provided the kids. Banks found himself being cared for by an indifferent staff who couldn't be bothered to teach him basic skills like cooking, let alone give him the love and guidance he was seeking. "It was like having blind or dead babysitters," he writes. Banks argues that group homes need dedicated and accountable staff who can teach the residents such basic skills as money management, conflict resolution, and job interview techniques.

Coming into the system at age 10, people told me all types of stuff about the bullies, the thieves and the lack of freedom. All this was true. Living in a boys group home was like living in a scared straight program. What nobody warned me about, though, was how unprepared I'd be to face life on my own after living in one of those homes for seven years.

I was nervous when I came into the group home, but I hoped it would teach me to be responsible in a grown-up kind of way and change me into a better person.

The group home rewarded us with snacks and later bedtimes when we showed we could handle chores like vacuuming, washing dishes and cleaning the bathroom without being asked. I was angry for having my freedom taken away, but after awhile, I felt I was becoming more mature. All the bad things people told me about group homes made me want to do what I had to so I could get out quicker.

A "Don't Care" Attitude

A few months later, though, all the staff who really cared for us left or found better jobs. The new staff wasn't experienced with

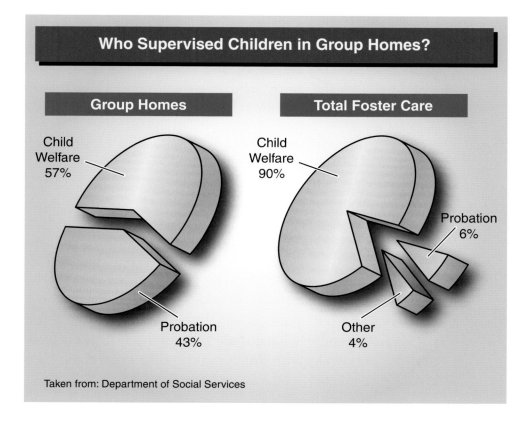

Who Supervised Children in Group Homes?

Group Homes

Child Welfare 57%

Probation 43%

Total Foster Care

Child Welfare 90%

Probation 6%

Other 4%

Taken from: Department of Social Services

adolescents and had an "I don't give a damn about these kids just give me my paycheck" attitude. Since our parents weren't around, I felt it was their job to be our parents. Their jobs are not like working a register: If you're not built for the challenge or don't care for us, then don't waste our time.

But they stayed, making my life hard. If I asked their advice, they would always tell me to talk to my social worker, who came in only three days a week and always missed meetings with me. If I was depressed about something, like a home visit being cancelled or a visit that went bad, they wouldn't sit down and talk to me to find out what was wrong or if I was all right. It was like having blind or dead babysitters.

No one ever talked to me about going to college or vocational school, how to have a career, how to rent and keep an apartment, how to resolve conflicts with people or even how to cook a hamburger all the way through.

Cooking should have been easy to teach since the staff cooked every day. But when I asked to be taught they'd say, "Y'all know we don't allow y'all thieving asses to be in this kitchen." They didn't want us in the kitchen because most of the residents would steal food from the pantry. The only thing that I know how to cook today is fried fish, grilled cheese sandwiches and those little packs of soup.

An Inferior Education

Let's talk about the group home school I had to go to up there, too. They would teach us way below regular standards. In 10th grade math class, I was assigned fractions that I learned in the 7th grade.

One day, I came home on a visit and saw my 12-year-old brother doing his homework at the living room table. "What kind of work you doing?" I asked him.

"Math," he said. He handed me his worksheet. It was polynomials (a form of algebra), which was the same exact thing I was getting in 10th grade at the group home.

Jim Gannaway, of Casey Family Services, is among those who are working on programs to help teens prepare for life outside the foster care system.

Worse, he was doing it with no problem. It was easy for him! I had a hard time finding a formula for a bunch of letters and numbers. I really got upset thinking what my life would be like when I left the group home.

Making Mistakes

When I eventually got discharged, I desperately needed a job. I didn't know what was needed for a job interview besides a tie, slacks and a dress shirt. I went on three job interviews and was turned away each time because I didn't have something that I didn't know I needed.

First, it was a state ID that I didn't have. I got one. The second time it was a Social Security card I didn't have. I got that. The third time I was turned down because I didn't bring my birth certificate. I got that, too—but I felt five steps behind, not knowing something that everyone else seemed to know.

This is how I've had to learn-by rejection and making mistakes. I feel we should be taught what to expect ahead of time. I want to be prepared for what's coming up so I don't have to ask for help.

If I were in charge of a group home, I would try to make living there more like real life. I'd try to make sure every discharged resident is properly prepared for society instead of feeling left behind and not ready.

What I Would Change

The group home would teach things residents need to know to be independent after leaving care—how to manage money, make a budget and keep a job. Young people would be taught how to cook, clean, get along with people and pay bills. I would try to get people who could offer job opportunities involved with the agency so residents would have jobs to go to after they leave.

When a resident gets discharged, he would be able to keep in touch and visit the group home to learn more skills to deal with obstacles he faces.

I would only hire qualified staff who love kids. That way, residents who feel stressed, angry, or lonely would have staff who are willing to listen, be supportive and help them through the hardship of being away from their families.

I feel it's the system's responsibility to hire good staff. Every two or three months, I'd have residents rate the staff so that everyone knows which staff members are good for the kids and the agency.

The staff who the residents rate highest would receive pay raises to reduce the chance of them leaving to find better paying jobs. That way, the good staff will get good pay and the residents will be better prepared for society when they leave.

What You Should Know About Foster Care

Foster Care Facts

- More than five hundred thousand American children are in foster care.
- The most common reasons children are removed from their homes are general neglect, physical abuse, and sexual abuse.
- The average age of a child in foster care is 10.1 years.
- The median age of kids in foster care who are waiting to be adopted is 7.8 years.
- Fifty-three percent of children in foster care are male and 47% are female.
- The mean length a child will stay in foster care is twenty months, but children can stay in the system for years.
- Almost 70% of children waiting to be adopted have been in continuous foster care for two years or more. Twenty-five percent have been in for five years or more.
- It costs taxpayers approximately $3000 a month to place a child in foster care. Foster care families receive only a fraction of this. In Rhode Island, foster care families receive about $13.64 a day to take care of a four- to eleven-year-old child.
- Minority children are overrepresented in the foster care population. Minority children make up 33% of the U.S. population, but 55% of the foster care population.
- Many children in the foster care system have physical or psychological problems. These can be caused by a host of factors including: prenatal drug or alcohol use, neglect, abuse, and multiple foster care placements.

- Adolescents living with foster parents or in group homes have about four times the rate of serious psychiatric disorders than do those living with their own families.
- Thirty to 40% of children in the child welfare system have physical health problems.
- More than 2 million U.S. children live with their grandparents or other relatives because their parents cannot care for them.
- Kids in foster care often struggle with the following issues: blaming themselves for their removal from their birth parents, wanting to return to parents even if the parents were abusive, feeling unwanted, feeling helpless about being switched to different families, feeling confused about whether they should become attached to foster families, and feeling insecure about their futures.

Leaving Foster Care

- Most children who are placed in foster care are put there only temporarily.
- About 22% of children in foster care are available for adoption.
- When foster kids leave foster care, most (60%) are reunited with their parents. Thirteen percent go to live with other relatives, and 12% are adopted.
- Seventy-five percent of single women adopting an unrelated foster child choose an African American child. Single women are also more likely to adopt an older foster child.
- Foster children have the most chance of being adopted by their foster parents (64%). Twenty percent are adopted by nonrelatives and 16% by relatives.
- A disproportionate number of children aged one to five are adopted. When a child reaches age eight or nine, it is more likely that he or she will remain in foster care than be adopted.
- Sixty percent of children waiting to be adopted are six years or older.
- A child is most likely to be adopted six to eleven months after the birth parents' rights were terminated.

- There are two and a half times more children waiting to be adopted than the number of children who are adopted.

Life After Foster Care
- Twenty thousand foster care kids will reach age eighteen this year, thus aging out of the system.
- Only 60% complete high school.
- Only 2% get a college degree.
- Eight-four percent will become a parent twelve to eighteen months after aging out.
- Fifty-one percent are unemployed.
- Thirty percent have no health insurance.
- Twenty-five percent will spend some time being homeless.
- Thirty percent will be on public assistance.
- Thirty percent of the nation's homeless report a history in foster care.

What You Should Do About Foster Care

It is rare to find a person who would argue that the foster care system is perfect the way it is. The issues surrounding the foster care system are too complex for that. The real debates about foster care center around particular issues, such as how to solve the problems that kids face in the foster care system and how the system should be structured. Foster care is a unique issue in that it will never be completely "solved." No matter how well parents are educated, no matter what laws are made, no matter how the problem is approached, there are always going to be children who—for one reason or another—cannot live with their parents. The real goal, then, is to figure out a way to care for these children in the best way possible.

The Problems of the Foster Care System

The foster care system was designed with good intentions—it was a way to help and find homes for homeless, abused, and orphaned children. But in many ways the system isn't working. Opponents of the foster care system can list a host of problems. Too many children end up languishing in foster care for years. Children can be shuffled around from home to home, leaving them with no sense of stability. Kids from minority families are overrepresented in the foster care system. And kids beyond about the age of six have little chance of being adopted. The people who care for foster children are not paid enough to cover the children's basic needs. Foster children often don't receive proper medical care and children with special needs often don't get the services for their conditions. Foster children can be subject to sexual or physical abuse or neglect from foster parents.

There is not enough training for children who leave the foster care system at age eighteen, to help them deal with life on their own. And there is minimal support for foster kids once they leave foster care. Those teenagers who "age out" of the system face an uncertain future. They are likely to become homeless at some point, receive government assistance, and have children of their own at young age. They are unlikely to finish high school and even less likely to go to college.

Issues in Foster Care

If you want to do something about the foster care system, the best way to start is to figure out which issue is most important to you. If there is a particular issue you feel passionately about, that is the one to focus on because your passion will fuel your energy to tackle the problem. Even though the foster care system has been around in the United States for centuries, there are still plenty of debates raging about the topic. Is it better, for example, for a child from an abusive family to be placed in foster care or for the family to be educated in parenting techniques so that family can stay together? Are group homes a good idea for housing older kids? What sort of oversight should foster care parents be subject to? How can people be encouraged to adopt older children and those with special needs? What is the best way to provide foster kids with the proper tools for a better future?

How to Help

The most direct way to help a foster child is to adopt him or her. By talking about foster care with people you know, you might inspire someone to take on a child. If someone you know expresses interest in fostering or adopting a child, direct them to agencies, books, or Web sites where they can learn more about the issue.

Foster care agencies and children's homes often need donations. You could organize a drive to collect toys, clothes, shoes, and books to give to the children. Check your local phone book to find local agencies and call them to see what they need. You can also volunteer your time at a children's home. They might want someone to help with the younger kids or maybe someone to read to them. Just showing up on a regular basis to play games with younger children will provide them with more of a sense of continuity. One of the best ways to help foster kids is to help them get an education. You can donate school supplies, help them with their homework, or even start a scholarship fund. You can also collect money for particular "extra" costs like going to camp, buying a prom dress, or getting a yearbook.

If you want to advocate for a particular issue, write letters to the editor of the local paper. Write an editorial for your school newspaper. Look online to find advocacy groups and contact some to find out how you can help. Talk about your issue with people you know and encourage them to take action, too.

If You Know Someone in Foster Care
Foster kids sometimes feel stigmatized for being a foster child. The best way to help them is simply to be friendly and let them see that you like them regardless of what their housing status is. A good, loyal friend is probably what they need the most. If it seems appropriate, you might figure out what kind of help your friend might need. Perhaps your family could offer him or her rides to sporting events or you might invite them along on family outings.

If You Are in Foster Care
The most important thing to remember is that being in foster care is not your fault. It might be helpful to connect with other kids in the same situation. One of the best way to find how other kids are dealing with foster care is by reading *Represent* magazine (www.youthcomm.org). It is written by kids in foster care and

covers just about every issue foster kids deal with. You can also find out what services are available to you and take advantage of them. If there is a service you need, don't be afraid to ask. If you have access to a computer, look online for foster care information and services. And if you are getting ready to age out of the system, locate an alumni group. (A prominent one is Foster Care Alumni of America at www.fostercarealumni.org.) Such a group will provide you with information and, most importantly, a group of mentors who are looking forward to helping you.

ORGANIZATIONS TO CONTACT

American Foster Care Resources (AFCR)
PO Box 271, King George, VA 22485
(540) 775-7410 • fax: (540)775-3271
e-mail:afcr@afcr.com • Web site: www.afcr.com

AFCR is dedicated to the research, development, and production of informational and educational resources for and about family foster care. AFCR provides resource materials to foster care providers, the children in care and their families, and the placing agency's staff and administration. AFCR publishes *Foster Care Journal.*

Association of Administrators of the Interstate Compact for the Placement of Children (AAICPC)
American Public Human Services Association, 810 First St. NE, Suite 500, Washington, DC 20002-4267
(202) 682-0100 • fax: (202) 289-6555
e-mail: icpcinbox@aphsa.org • Web site: http://icpc.aphsa.org

The Interstate Compact for the Placement of Children is a uniform state law establishing a contract among party states to ensure that children placed across state lines receive adequate protection and services. The primary function of the ICPC is to protect the interests of both the children and the states by requiring that certain procedures be followed in the interstate placement of children who are being adopted, placed with relatives, or going into residential care or foster family homes.

Center for Child and Family Programs
Institute for the Study of Children, Families, and Communities/CCFP 203 Boone Hall, Eastern Michagan University, Ypsilanti, MI 48197
(734) 487-0372 • fax: (734) 487-0284
e-mail: vpolakow@online.emich.edu • Web site: http://www.iscfc.emich.edu

The goals of the Center for Child and Family Programs, formerly the National Foster Care Resource Center, are to enhance the lives of vulnerable children and families and to shape local, state, and national policies by working with public and private agencies to conduct research about vulnerable children and families, demonstrate new models of service, develop training curricula, provide training and technical assistance, conduct program evaluations, and develop policy recommendations.

Center for Family Connections (CFFC)
350 Cambridge St., Cambridge, MA 02141
(617) 547-0909 • toll-free: (800) KINNECT • fax: (617) 497-5952
e-mail: cffc@kinnect.org • Web site: www.kinnect.org/

The goal of the Center for Family Connections is to serve individuals and families touched by adoption, foster care, kinship, and guardianship, as well as other complex blended families, and to serve the people with whom they are connected by offering training, education, consultation, advocacy, and clinical treatment.

Child Welfare League of America (CWLA)
440 First St., NW, 3rd Fl., Washington, DC 20001-2085
(202) 638-2952 • fax: (202) 638-4004
e-mail: fostercare@cwla.org • Web site: www.cwla.org

CWLA is an association of nearly eight hundred public and private nonprofit agencies that assist more than 3.5 million abused and neglected children and their families each year with a range of services, including policy advocacy and creating the "Child Welfare Standards of Excellence." It publishes *Children's Voice* and *Child Welfare Journal*.

Foster Care Alumni of America (FCAA)
16 E. Main St., Richmond, VA 23219
(804) 649-3222 • toll-free: (888) 258-6640 • fax: (804) 649-3223
e-mail: admin@fostercarealumni.org • Web site: www.fostercare alumni.org

Foster Care Alumni of America is a national independent non-profit organization founded and led by alumni of the foster care system. FCAA provides opportunities for alumni of foster care to join together and to use their experiences and power to effect positive change. The group believes that lasting change happens when alumni have opportunities to connect with each other to advocate for better futures for people in and from foster care.

Foster Family-Based Treatment Association (FFTA)
294 Union St., Hackensack, NJ 07601-4303
(800) 414-FFTA (-3382) • fax: (201) 489-4593
e-mail:ffta@ffta.org • Web site: www.ffta.org
The Foster Family-Based Treatment Association is a membership organization committed to enhancing the lives of children and their families by strengthening family-based organizations. Treatment foster care is a model of care that provides children with a combination of traditional foster care and residential treatment centers, with the treatment occurring within the foster family home.

Foster Grandparent Program (FGP)
7400 Laurel Hill Oaks Cir., Orlando, FL 32818
(407) 298-4180 • fax: (407) 298-2725
e-mail: fgpcf@fostergrandparentprogram.org • Web site: www.fostergrandparentprogram.org/foster_grandpx.html
A program matching volunteers—low-income people aged sixty and over—with children with special or exceptional needs. Volunteers work in schools and hospitals for retarded, disturbed, and handicapped children, day care centers, correctional institutions, city hospital wards, and other settings. Responsibilities include assisting in physical or speech therapy, teaching parenting skills, feeding and dressing the children, and providing emotional support.

Fostering Results
Children & Family Research Center, 150 N. Wacker Dr., Suite 2120, Chicago, IL 60606
(312) 641-2505 • fax: (312) 641-2337
e-mail: fosteringresults@uiuc.edu • Web site: www.fostering results.org

Fostering Results was launched by a grant from the Pew Charitable Trusts to create a public education campaign regarding foster care. Its mission is to engage influential national and local leaders; judges; child welfare directors and caseworkers; and advocates for youth and foster, birth, and adoptive families, using media, reports, and meetings to call attention to the financing and court issues at the heart of the foster care system recommendations crafted by the Pew Commission on Children in Foster Care.

National Association of Former Foster Care Children of America (NAFFCCA)

680 Rhode Island Ave. NE, Suite H-7, Washington, DC 20002
(202) 635-7610 • fax: (202) 635-7622
e-mail: info@naffcca.org • Web site: www.naffcca.org

Advocates for the needs of children in foster care. Provides children and youth from foster care with the life skills necessary to become fully independent, healthy, and productive members of society. Assists teens in transitioning from being in foster care to being an independent adult.

National Foster Parent Association (NFPA)

7512 Stanich Ave., No. 6, Gig Harbor, WA 98335
(253) 853-4000 • toll-free: (800) 557-5238 • fax: (253) 853-4001

The NFPA seeks to identify and advocate for the needs of children in foster care and those who care for them. The group offers technical assistance and organizational-skills training to state and local foster parent associations. NFPA works to improve the foster parenting image nationwide and to educate the courts, legislators, and the public to the needs of children in the foster care system. It informs foster parents of their legal rights, encourages mandatory parenting skills training, and a minimum requirement of preservice training for all foster parents.

Orphan Foundation of America
21351 Gentry Dr., Unit 130, Sterling, VA 20166
(571) 203-0270 • fax: (571) 203-0273
e-mail: help@orphan.org • Web site: www.orphan.org

The Orphan Foundation of America's mission is to provide opportunities for America's foster youth to continue their education, to increase awareness of the number and plight of older teens leaving the bureaucratic maze of foster care, to highlight the potential of America's foster youth and the importance of supporting their dreams, and to offer direct opportunities for citizens, business, and civic organizations to assist older foster youth.

Partners in Foster Care
PO Box 2534, Madison, WI 53701
(608) 274-9111
e-mail: cwhite@fostering.us • Web site: www.fostering.us

Seeks to improve the lives of foster children through an alliance between private individuals and business leaders. Supports foster and adoptive families and the children living in their homes. Provides social, cultural, and educational activities to disadvantaged, medically fragile, abused, and neglected children living in out-of-home care.

Youth Communication
224 W. Twenty-ninth St., New York, NY 10001
212-279-0708 • fax: 212-279-8856
e-mail: info@youthcomm.org • Web site: www.youthcomm.org

Youth Communication helps teenagers develop their skills in reading, writing, thinking, and reflection so they can acquire the information they need to make thoughtful choices about their lives. It publishes books and periodicals, including *Represent*, a magazine written by kids in foster care for kids in foster care.

BIBLIOGRAPHY

Books

Elizabeth Bartholet, *Nobody's Children: Abuse and Neglect, Foster Drift, and the Adoption Alternative.* Boston: Beacon, 1999.

Nina Bernstein, *The Lost Children of Wilder: The Epic Struggle to Change Foster Care.* New York: Pantheon, 2001.

Theresa Cameron, *Foster Care Odyssey: A Black Girl's Story.* Jackson: University Press of Mississippi, 2002.

Al Desetta, ed., *The Heart Knows Something Different: Teenage Voices from the Foster Care System.* New York: Youth Communication, 1996.

Al Desetta, ed., *In the System and in the Life: A Guide for Teens and Staff to the Gay Experience in Foster Care.* New York: Youth Communication, 2003.

Dahveed, *Through the Eyes of a Foster Child.* Bloomington, IN: Authorhouse, 2005.

Paul E. Knowlton, *The Original Foster Care Survival Guide.* Lincoln, NE: iUniverse, 2005.

Betsy Krebs and Paul Pitcoff, *Beyond the Foster Care System: The Future for Teens.* Piscataway, NJ: Rutgers University Press, 2006.

C. McKelvey and J. Stevens, *Adoption Crisis: The Truth Behind Adoption and Foster Care.* Golden, CO: Fulcrum, 1995.

Dorothy Roberts, *Shattered Bonds: The Color of Child Welfare.* New York: Basic Books, 2002.

M. Shirk and G. Stangler, *On Their Own: What Happens to Kids When They Age Out of the Foster Care System.* Boulder, CO: Westview, 2004.

Ian Sinclair, *Foster Children: Where They Go and How They Get On.* London: Jessica Kingsley, 2005.

Beatrice Sparks, *Finding Katie: The Diary of Anonymous, a Teenager in Foster Care*. New York: HarperCollins, 2005.

Periodicals

Amanda Bowers, "Sharing Family Values," *Time*, February 17, 2003.

Debera Carlton Harrell, "Grandparent Caregivers Seek Help from Rest of the 'Village,'" *Seattle-Post Intelligencer*, July 6, 2002.

Gregory K. Fritz, "How to Improve Foster-Care 'System,'" *Providence (RI) Journal*, June 5, 2004.

John Iwasaki, "Partnership Is All About What's Best For At-Risk Children," *Seattle Post-Intelligencer*, March 14, 2007.

Olympian, "Foster Kids Merit Further Support," Feburary 12, 2006.

Kim Pittaway, "Pretending We Care," *Chatelaine*, May 2001.

Natasha Santos, "No Easy Answers," *New York Daily News*, January 30, 2006.

Carol Spigner, "Tailor Foster Care to Individuals' Needs," *USA Today*, January 29, 2004.

Andrew White, "More Foster Care Won't Reduce Deaths," *New York Daily News*, November 27, 2005.

Internet Sources

Marvena Brown, "Abuse Creates Special Challenges," *Sacramento (CA) Bee*, June 12, 2001. www.sacbee.com/static/archive/news/projects/foster/20010612main.html.

Dominick Freeman, "Finding My Father: My Dream Dad Turned Out to Be Gay," *Represent*, November/December, 2005. www.youthcomm.org/FCYU-Features/NovDec2005/FCYU-2005-11-04b.htm.

Ellen Herman, "Fostering and Foster Care," Adoption History Project, Feburary, 2005. http://darkwing.uoregon.edu/~adoption/topics/fostering.htm.

Christine Korn, "Grandparents Can Make the Difference in Child Protection Crisis," *Senior Journal.com*, May 9, 2006. www. seniorjournal.com/NEWS/(Grandparents/5-09-06Grand parentsMakeDifference.htm.

Miriam Aroni Krinsky and Donna M. Butts, "Out of the Foster-Care Lifeboat," *SFGate.com*, February 14, 2006. www.sfgate.com/cgi-bin/article.cgi?f=/c/a/2006/02/14/EDGU9GJDUU1.DTL.

Aquellah Mahdi, "Learning to Love Again: I Finally Found a Foster Mom I Can Trust," *Represent*, July/August 2006. www.youth comm.org/FCYU-Features/JulyAug2006/2006-07-04b.htm.

Dale Margolin, "What You Should Know Before You Leave the System," *Represent*, January/February, 2007. www.youthcomm .org/FCYU-Features/JanFeb2007/2007-01-08b.htm.

Carlos R. Moreno, "A Call to Action on Foster Children," *SFGate. com*, April 20, 2006. www.sfgate.com/cgi-bin/article.cgi?file=/chronicle/archive/2006/04/20/EDGNSGUBOG1.DTL.

Jennifer Roback Morse, "Languishing in Foster Care?" Townhall. com, March 13, 2006. www.townhall.com/columnists/JenniferR obackMorse/2006/03/13/languishing_in_foster_care.

Jessica Wiggs, "An Angel from Above: My Grandma Put Her Life on Hold to Raise Us," *Represent*, January/February, 2006. www. youthcomm.org/FCYU-Features/JanFeb2006/FCYU-2006-01 -04b.htm.